Slow Cook

50 Flavorous and Easy Recipes for Two

Jane Willan

Copyright 2017

Your Free Gift

I wanted to show my appreciation that you support my work so I've put together a free gift for you.

Big Diabetic Cookbook:
101 Diabetic Recipes for Living Well with Type 2 Diabetes

Just visit the link above to download it now.

I know you will love this gift.

Thanks!

Table of Contents:

Introduction

Stew of frozen vegetables and beef

Vegetable ragout with tuna

Ribs with spices and orange juice

Pita with meat and vegetables

Ragout of vegetables and smoked sausage

Chicken with spices

Warming cocktail with spices

Chicken Stew with Rice and Shrimps

Stew with meatballs

Sirloin fillet with sesame seeds

Ragout of meat, vegetables and pearl barley

Pork soup

Ragout of beef with beans

Bean spreads

Chicken thighs with carrots

Beef stewed with vegetables

Bean stew with meatballs

Salmon in ginger broth

Garnish of beets and shallots

Vegetable stew with beans and corn

Meat ragout with vegetables

Pork ribs with beans

Chicken wings

Spicy chicken wings

Burgers with stewed meat

Beef with potatoes and rosemary

Vegetable stew with rice

Lamb, stewed with beans and artichokes

Lamb cooked with vegetables and pearl barley

Chicken fillet

Cheese appetizer

Chicken soup with zucchini and lentils

Tomato sauce for pasta

Asian chicken noodle soup

Sword fish with BBQ sauce

Beef tenderloin

Spaghetti with meat sauce in Italian

Stew of beef and black beans

Beef with cabbage, carrots and pasta

Chicken stewed in tomato sauce

Paprikash with noodles

Meat

Sandwiches from ciabatta, chicken fillet and vegetables

Ragout of pumpkin with turkey

Stew with chicken

Stew of vegetables and meat

Chicken fillet stewed with vegetables

Chicken Stewed with Vegetables and Herbs

Spicy beef with vegetables

Sandwich with beef brisket and mushrooms

Introduction

You bought Slow Cooker and what and how can you cook in it until you know? With the help of our book you can not only quickly cook delicious dishes, but also turn the cooking process into a real treat. Crockpot chicken, Salmon in ginger broth and Vegetable ragout with tuna, soups and cereals, cooked according to our recipes, will be not only tasty, but also useful. Create your own recipes. Bon Appetite!

Stew of frozen vegetables and beef

Ingredients:
- Beef tenderloin - 450 g
- Chili powder - 1-2 teaspoons
- Vegetable oil
- A mixture of frozen vegetables - 450 g
- Corn frozen - 1 glass
- Salsa vegetable - 450 g
- Water - 1/2 cup
- Salt to taste

Preparation:
1. Remove the fat from the meat and cut the flesh into pieces 2.5 cm in size. Put the beef in a bowl, sprinkle with chili and mix well.
2. With a large frying pan, sprinkle with vegetable oil and heat on medium-high heat. Put half the whole cut meat on a heated frying pan and fry, stirring, until brown on all sides. Transfer the fried meat to a plate, put the remaining beef in the pan and brown it too.
3. Add frozen vegetables and corn to the bowl of a large slow cooker, top the roasted meat, pour the vegetable salsa and water.
4. Close the slow-cooker and cook the stew at a slow power of 8-9 hours, or at a strong power - 4-4.5 hours. Before serving, add salt to taste.
The finished stew is served in a bowl immediately.

Vegetable ragout with tuna

Ingredients:
- Olive oil - 30 g
- Onion - 1 piece
- Garlic - 1 piece
- White dry wine - 75 g
- Tomatoes, canned without a skin - 200 g
- Vegetable or fish broth, boiling water - 150 g
- Paprika - 1 teaspoon
- Chili powder dried, crumbled - 1/2 teaspoon
- Potatoes - 450 g
- Pepper Bulgarian red - 1 piece
- Pepper Bulgarian yellow - 1 piece
- A branch of fresh rosemary
- Bay leaf - 1 piece
- Tuna fillet - 450 g
- Salt and black ground pepper
- Home baked bread

Preparation:

1. Heat olive oil in a large frying pan. Pour the onion into a heated frying pan and fry, stirring, for about 10 minutes, until soft. Then add garlic in the pan, add wine, broth, put tomatoes, sprinkle with paprika and chili. On medium heat bring the mass to a boil, and then transfer this mass into a slow-blowing bowl.
2. Add potatoes, bell peppers, rosemary and bay leaves to vegetables, mix well. Close the slow-cooker and cook the vegetables for about 2-2.5 hours, until the potato is soft, then add salt and pepper the vegetables to taste.
3. Put the pieces of tuna on the vegetables, cover the slow cooker with a lid and cook for another 15-20 minutes, until the fish is ready.
4. Remove the bay leaf and rosemary sprig from the stew, and serve immediately.

Ribs with spices and orange juice

Ingredients:
- Beef ribs - 1,8-2,2 kg
- Leek - 3 pieces
- Garlic - 6 pieces
- Ginger - 2.5 cm
- Anise - 1 piece
- Dried chili pepper - 1 piece
- Dry wine or beef broth - 0.5 cups
- Orange Juice - 0.5 cups
- Soy sauce - 0,25 cup
- Orange peel - 4 pieces
- Brown sugar - 2 tablespoons
- Parsley - 0.5 beam
- Salt - 1,5 teaspoons
- Pepper black ground - 0.5 teaspoon

Preparation:
1. Cut the beef ribs into several pieces. Peel onion and cut into pieces 5 cm long. Cut the garlic into plates. Ginger clean and cut into plates too. Anise breaks into pieces. Chopped parsley.
2. Place the ribs on a baking sheet, sprinkle with salt and pepper. Bake (preferably with top heat) for 10 minutes, until golden brown.
3. In a ceramic form for slow-cook, lay out the leek. On top lay out the ribs. Add the garlic, ginger, anise and chili.
4. In a bowl, mix the wine (or beef broth), zest, orange juice, soy sauce and brown sugar. Drizzle with a mixture of ribs. Cover and put in the refrigerator for the night.
5. Put the shape in a slow-blower. Close and cook at low power 11-12 hours or with strong power 5.5-6 hours.
6. Remove the ribs from the plate, cover and keep warm. Remove fat from gravy.
7. Serve beef ribs, sprinkle with parsley and sprinkle with gravy.

Pita with meat and vegetables

Ingredients:
- Beef spatula - 600-900 g
- Lemon pepper - 1/2 teaspoon
- Mustard powder - 1/2 teaspoon
- Chicken broth - 1/2 cup
- Lemon peel - 1/4 teaspoon
- Lemon juice - 1 tablespoon
- Fresh rosemary - 1 teaspoon
- Garlic - 2 slices
- Natural yoghurt - 1/2 cup
- Fresh cucumber - 1/4 cup
- Lemon pepper - 1/4 teaspoon
- Pita from whole wheat flour - 3 pieces
- Salad leaves - 6 pieces
- Fresh tomato - 1 piece

Preparation:
1. Cut the meat into pieces so that it fits in the medium slow-blower. In a small bowl, mix 1/2 teaspoon of lemon pepper and mustard powder. Grate this mixture with meat and combine it into a slow-blowing bowl. In a small bowl, mix the broth, lemon zest, juice, rosemary and garlic. Pour this mixture of meat in a slow cooker.
2. Close the slow-cooker and cook meat at a slow power for 8-10 hours, or for strong power - 4-5 hours.
3. In another small bowl, mix the yogurt, cucumber and 1/4 teaspoon of lemon pepper. Put the sauce aside.
4. Take the meat from the slow-cooker. With two forks, tear the meat into small pieces.
5. Each half of the pita is lined with lettuce leaves, stuffed with meat, tomatoes and pour a snack of pita with yoghurt sauce.

Ragout of vegetables and smoked sausage

Ingredients:
- Potatoes young small - 230 g
- Carrots of medium size - 3 pieces
- Onions - 1 piece
- Smoked sausage - 450 g
- Beer strong or non-alcoholic - 300 g
- Chicken broth - 1 glass
- Paprika - 1/2 teaspoon
- Seeds of cumin - 1/2 teaspoon
- Black pepper - 1/2 teaspoon
- Sauerkraut - 400 g
- Spaghetti boiled hot - 3 cups
- Mustard whole meal

Preparation:
1. Put the potatoes, carrots and onions in a bowl of a large slow-cooker. Top with sausage.
2. In a medium-sized bowl, mix the beer, broth, paprika, cumin and pepper. Pour this spicy brew the contents of the slow-cooker, top the cabbage.
3. Close the slow-cooker and cook the dish at a slow capacity about 7-9 hours or at a strong power of 3.5-4.5 hours.
4. Put the spaghetti in the serving plates, and put a stew on them with noise. If desired, you can pour the dish with the juice that was formed during the preparation of the stew. It is good to serve mustard with this dish.

Chicken with spices

Ingredients:
- Chicken thighs without bone and skins - 24-30 pieces
- Onion - 2 cups
- Tapioca fast food - 0,25 cups
- Garlic - 8 teeth
- Cumin ground - 1 tablespoon
- Curry powder - 2 teaspoons
- Ground coriander - 1.5 teaspoons
- Cinnamon ground - 0.5 teaspoon
- Carnation ground - 0.25 teaspoons
- Cayenne pepper powder - 0.25 teaspoons
- Broth chicken - 400 g
- Natural yogurt without additives - 180 g
- Rice cooked - 3 cups
- Salt
- Black pepper powder

Preparation:
1. Put onion in a large slow-cooker, sprinkle with tapioca and garlic. Top out with chicken thighs. Sprinkle with cumin, curry, coriander, cinnamon, cloves, cayenne pepper, 1.5 teaspoons of salt and 0.25 teaspoons of pepper. Pour the contents of the slower broth with the broth, close the lid and cook at a slow power for about 7-8 hours.
2. Chicken thighs get from the slow-cooker, lay out on a serving dish. In the slow cooker with onions add yogurt, mix well. Serve this onion sauce with thighs and boiled rice.

Warming cocktail with spices

Ingredients:
- Orange - 1 piece
- Lemon - 1 piece
- Slices of fresh ginger - 4 pieces
- Cinnamon stick - 7.5 cm
- Sweet pepper - 8 peas
- Carnation - 8 buds
- Bordeaux wine 750 g
- Water - 4 cups
- Concentrated pineapple juice - 350 g
- Brandy - 1/2 cup
- Sugar - 1/2 cup
- Orange liqueur - 1/4 cup
- Orange slices and cinnamon sticks

Preparation:
1. With the help of vegetable peeler remove from the citrus a few strips of peel. Squeeze out the citrus juice and pour into a small bowl.
2. From several layers of gauze, add a square, measuring 15x15 cm. Put citrus peel, ginger, a broken cinnamon stick, sweet pepper and cloves into the center of the square. Collapse the gauze with a bag and tie the thread.
3. Put a bag of spices in the bowl of a large slow-cooker, pour wine, water, pineapple juice, brandy, orange liqueur and citrus juice, pour sugar and close the slow-cooker. Cook at a slow power for 4-5 hours or at a strong power of 2-2 1/2 hours.
4. Then open the slow-blower, remove the bag of spices, and pour the drink into serving glasses and decorate with orange slices and / or cinnamon sticks. Of this amount of ingredients, approximately 22 servings of 110 grams are obtained.

Chicken Stew with Rice and Shrimps

Ingredients:
- Chicken fillet without skin - 450 g
- Celery stalk - 4 pieces
- Onion - 2 pieces
- Canned tomatoes, peeled - 400 g
- Chicken broth - 300 g
- Tomato paste - 90 g
- Garlic - 2 slices
- Salt - 1/2 teaspoon
- Brown rice - 1 1/2 cups
- Bulgarian pepper of any color - 3/4 cup
- Shrimp fresh or frozen - 230 g
- Fresh parsley - 2 tablespoons
- Celery leaves
- For a mixture of spices:
- White ground pepper - 1/4 teaspoon
- Garlic powder - 1/4 teaspoon
- Onion powder - 1/4 teaspoon
- Paprika powder - 1/4 teaspoon
- Black ground pepper - 1/4 teaspoon
- Red ground pepper - 1/8 teaspoon

Preparation:
1. In a small bowl, mix all the spices and set aside.
2. Chicken fillet cut into pieces 2 cm and folded into a bowl of a large slow-cooker. There also lay celery, onions, tomatoes, tomato paste, chopped garlic, pour the prepared mixture of spices, salt and pour everything with broth.
3. Close the slow-cooker and cook chicken ragout at low power 4 1/2-5 hours or at strong power 2 1/4-2 3/4 hours.
4. Put rice and Bulgarian pepper into a slow cooker, close the slow cooker and cook the chicken ragout at a strong power for about 30 minutes, until the rice is ready and the liquid is almost completely evaporated.
5. Before serving in the stew, add boiled shrimp and parsley. Serve chicken ragout in plate saucers, decorating with celery leaf.

Stew with meatballs

Ingredients:
- Tomatoes, preserved with spices - 700 g
- Poultry meatballs, freshly prepared or frozen - 350 g
- Red canned beans - 400 g
- Chicken broth with spices - 350 g
- Corn grains, fresh or frozen - 300 g
- Fresh Oregano

Preparation:
1. Put tomatoes, meatballs, beans, corn in a bowl of a large slow-cooker and pour everything with broth.
2. Close the slow-cooker and cook the dish at low power for 6-7 hours or at a strong power of 3-3.5 hours.
3. Serve the dish immediately with oregano leaves.

Sirloin fillet with sesame seeds

Ingredients:
- Turkey fillet - 1.4 kg
- Black ground pepper - 1/4 teaspoon
- Cayenne pepper - 1/8 teaspoon
- Chicken broth - 1/4 cup
- Soy sauce - 1/4 cup
- Fresh ginger - 4 teaspoons
- Fresh lemon juice - 1 tablespoon
- Sesame oil - 1 tablespoon
- Garlic - 2 slices
- Cornstarch - 2 tablespoons
- Cold water - 2 tablespoons
- Onion green - 2 tablespoons
- Sesame seeds - 1 tablespoon

Preparation:
1. Put the turkey fillet into a bowl of a large slow cooker. Sprinkle with cayenne and black pepper. In a small bowl, mix the broth, soy sauce, ginger, lemon juice, sesame oil and garlic. Pour this mixture of turkey in a slow cooker.
2. Close the slow-cooker and cook the turkey fillet at low power for 5-6 hours or at high 2 1 / 2-3 hours.
3. Transfer the fillets to the serving dish, reserving the liquid. Cover the turkey breast with foil to keep warm.
4. For the sauce, you must strain the liquid from the slow-blower through a sieve and pour it into the saucepan. In a small bowl, dilute the starch in cold water, put this mixture into a saucepan with sauce. Put the saucepan on medium heat and cook, stirring, until thick, about 3 minutes.
5. Cut the turkey fillet into slices and serve with sauce, sprinkled with sesame and green onions.

Ragout of meat, vegetables and pearl barley

Ingredients:
- Meat beef or lamb for fire - 350 g
- Vegetable oil odorless - 1 tablespoon
- Beef broth - 1,5 l
- Tomatoes, canned without a skin - 400 g
- Onion - 1 glass
- Potatoes or parsnips - 1 glass
- Vegetable mixture - 1 glass
- Pearl barley - 2/3 cup
- Stew of celery chopped
- Bay leaf - 1 piece
- Garlic - 2 slices
- Oregano or basil dried - 1 teaspoon
- Black ground pepper - 1/4 teaspoon

Preparation:
1. With meat cut the fat, if any, and cut the flesh into pieces of about 2.5 cm. In a large frying pan over medium heat, heat the vegetable oil, lay the meat and fry, stirring, until brown on all sides. Drain the formed fat.
2. Fold the meat in a large slow cooker, pour the broth, put the tomatoes, onion, potatoes, frozen vegetables, pearl barley, celery, bay leaves, garlic, oregano (basil) and pour black ground pepper.
3. Close the slow-cooker and cook meat stew with vegetables at low power for about 8-10 hours or at a strong power of 4-5 hours.

Pork soup

Ingredients:
- Pork shoulder-blade - 600 g
- Olive oil - 1 tablespoon
- Canned beans - 300 g
- Fresh tomatoes - 300 g
- Onion medium size - 1/2 cup
- Chili green canned - 100 g
- Garlic - 2 slices
- Cumin - 3/4 teaspoon
- Salt - 1/2 teaspoon
- Chicken broth - 350 g
- Fresh spinach leaves - 1 glass
- Lime juice - 2 teaspoons
- Sour cream and fresh cilantro

Preparation:
1. Cut the meat into pieces 1.5 cm. In a large frying pan, heat the olive oil over a moderately strong fire, lay out the meat and fry, stirring, until brown. Put the fried meat in a large slow cooker.
2. Add beans, tomatoes, onions, chili, garlic, cumin and salt to the meat. Pour all the broth.
3. Close the slow-cooker and cook the dish at low power for 6-7 hours or at high power for 3-4 hours.
4. Then add spinach leaves and lime juice to the slow cooker. Serve soup with sour cream and parsley leaves.

Ragout of beef with beans

Ingredients:
- Beef cooked - 900 g
- Black beans, cooked or canned - 800 g
- Canned tinned tomatoes - 500 g
- Water - 0.5 cups
- Onion - 1 piece
- Garlic - 1-2 pieces
- Ground cumin - 1 tablespoon
- Salt - 1 teaspoon
- Pepper black ground - 1-2 pinches
- Chili powder ground to taste
- Olive or vegetable oil - 1 tablespoon

Preparation:
1. We prepare products for meat stew with black beans.
2. Peel onion and chop. Garlic clean and crush.
3. Heat oil on a medium heat in a frying pan. Lay the onions and garlic, fry, stirring, 4-5 minutes.
4. Add chili, cumin, salt, pepper and beef. Fry 6-8 minutes, stirring to make the beef brown.
5. Lubricate the oil mill with oil. Lay out the meat mixture. Add beans, tomatoes and water. Cover. Cook for 8-10 hours at low power.
6. Mix thoroughly before serving.

Bean spreads

Ingredients:

- White canned beans (washed and drained) - 850 g
- Chicken broth - 1/2 cup
- Olive oil - 1 tbsp. l.
- Garlic (chopped) - 3 teeth
- Fresh marjoram (chopped) - 1 tsp.
- Fresh rosemary (chopped) - 1/2 teaspoon
- Black ground pepper - 1/8 teaspoon
- Olive oil
- Fresh leaves of rosemary
- Toasts, chips

Preparation:

. Add the beans to the bowl of the slow cooker, add the broth, add 1 tablespoon of olive oil, garlic, 1 teaspoon of marjoram, rosemary and black ground pepper.
. Close the slow-cooker and cook the beans at a slow power for about 3-4 hours.
Prepare the beans with a potato mash; put a bean snack in a serving bowl, sprinkle with olive oil and sprinkle with fresh leaves of rosemary. Such a snack of beans is good to serve with toasts, chips.

Chicken thighs with carrots

Ingredients:
- Chicken thighs without skins - 8 pieces
- Carrots - 240 g
- Onion - 1/2 cup
- Prunes without stones - 1/2 cup
- Chicken broth - 400 g
- Curry powder - 1.25 teaspoons
- Salt - 1/2 teaspoon
- Cinnamon powder - 1/2 teaspoon

Preparation:
1. Put carrots, onions and prunes in a bowl of slow cookers, pour everything with broth. Top with chicken thighs. In a small bowl, mix curry powder, salt and cinnamon, sprinkle with this mixture chicken thighs.
2. Close the slow-cooker and cook the chicken with carrots at a slow power for about 8-10 hours or at a strong power of 4-5 hours.
3. Stew the chicken with carrots in a bowl and cover to keep warm. And close the slow-blower and boil the juice on strong power for about 20 minutes. Serve stewed chicken with carrots, pouring sauce from a slow-cooker.

Beef stewed with vegetables

Ingredients:
- Beef tenderloin - 1,3 kg
- Salt
- Ground black pepper
- Vegetable oil - 1 tablespoon
- Onion - 1 piece
- Pasternak - 2 pieces
- Carrots - 2 pieces
- Seeds of dill - 1/2 teaspoon
- Seeds of cumin - 1/2 teaspoon
- Salt - 1/4 teaspoon
- Beef broth - 1/5 cup
- Vodka - 1/4 cup
- Sour cream 230 g
- Flour - 1/3 cup
- Water - 1/4 cup
- Fresh dill - 2 teaspoons
- Mustard - 1 teaspoon
- Horseradish - 1 teaspoon
- Black cabbage - 2 cups
- Mushrooms champignons - 1 glass
- Mashed potatoes freshly prepared - 3 cups

Preparation:
1. Remove the fat from the meat and cut the pulp into 2-3 parts so that it fits in the slow-blowing bowl. Sprinkle meat with salt and pepper from all sides. In a large frying pan on medium-high heat, heat the vegetable oil, put the meat on the heated frying pan and fry until brown on all sides. Formed fat to drain.
2. In a bowl of slow cookers, add onions, parsnips and carrots. Sprinkle the vegetables with dill seeds, caraway seeds and 1/4 teaspoon of salt, lay out the meat on the vegetables, pour everything with broth and vodka.
3. Close the slow-cooker and cook the dish at a low power for about 10 hours or at a strong power of about 5 hours.

4. In a small bowl, mix sour cream, flour, water, dill, mustard and horseradish. From the slow cooker grab about 1 cup of hot liquid and pour it into the sour cream mixture, stir well. Pour this whole mass into a slow-blower.
5. Put the cabbage and mushrooms in a slow cooker, close and cook at a strong power for about 30-60 minutes, until the sauce thickens and the soft state of the vegetables.
6. Put the meat on a cutting board, cut into slices. Serve beef stew with vegetables, watering the sauce. Garnish for beef stew with vegetables can be served with mashed potatoes.

Bean stew with meatballs

Ingredients:
- Tomatoes canned without a skin - 800 g
- Meatballs, ready-made, frozen - 400 g
- White canned beans - 400 g
- Water - 1/2 cup
- Pesto Basil - 1/4 cup
- Parmesan cheese - 1/2 cup

Preparation:
1. Put tomatoes, meatballs, beans, pesto into a slow-cooking bowl and pour everything over with water.
2. Close Slow cooker and cook stew of beans with meatballs on a slow power about 5-7 hours or on a strong power of 2.5-3.5 hours. Before serving, sprinkle a stew of beans with meatballs.

Salmon in ginger broth

Ingredients:
- Salmon fillet - 450 g
- Fresh ginger - 2.5 cm
- Broth vegetable, hot - 500 g
- Shallot - 4 pieces
- Garlic - 1 slice
- Lemon grass - 1 stem
- Chili pepper powder, flakes - 0.5 teaspoon
- Fish sauce - 1 tablespoon
- Sugar cane - 1 teaspoon

Preparation:
1. Filleted salmon fillets in a food film and put in a freezer for 30-40 minutes. Take the fillet from the freezer, remove the film, and remove the skin. Cut the fillets into cubes measuring 2.5 cm, remove the bones.
2. Put the pieces of fish in a saucepan, cover and leave at room temperature.
3. Meanwhile, the broth is poured into ceramic dishes, placed in a slow-cooker, turned on for heating at maximum power. Add soup, garlic, ginger, lemon grass, chili, fish sauce and sugar to the broth. Cover, cook for 2 hours.
4. Spice the fish into a spicy broth, cook for 15 minutes. Turn off the slow-blower; leave the fish in it for 10-15 minutes.

Garnish of beets and shallots

Ingredients:
- Beetroots - 700 g
- Shallot - 2 tablespoons
- Red wine vinegar - 1,5 tablespoons
- Extra virgin olive oil - 1 tablespoon
- Dijon mustard - 1/2 teaspoon
- Black ground pepper - 1/4 teaspoon
- Salt - 1/8 teaspoon
- Parsley

Preparation:
1. Beetroot is wrapped in foil or parchment and cooked in a microwave oven until soft, for about 7 minutes. Let the beet stand at room temperature for 5 minutes, and then cut into slices.
2. In a large bowl combine shallots, red wine vinegar, olive oil, mustard, salt and black ground pepper, lightly beat with a fork. In this dressing, put the beets, mix. Sprinkle garnish from the beet with parsley.

Vegetable stew with beans and corn

Ingredients:
- Medium-sized zucchini - 1 piece
- Pepper Bulgarian green - 3/4 cup
- Onion medium size - 1 piece
- Celery stalk - 1 piece
- Chili powder - 2 teaspoons
- Oregano dried - 1 teaspoon
- Cumin ground - 1/2 teaspoon
- Tomatoes without a skin - 800 g
- Red beans, canned - 450 g
- Corn frozen - 300 g
- Vegetable salsa - 1 glass
- Cheddar Cheese - 3/4 cup
- Sour cream

Preparation:
1. In a large slow cooker, add the zucchini, bell pepper, onions, celery, pour the powder of chili, oregano and cumin, mix. Add the tomatoes, beans, corn and salsa, mix.
2. Close the slow-cooker and cook the vegetable stew at low power for 8-10 hours or at strong power for 4-5 hours. Serve the vegetable stew in a serving dish with sour cream, sprinkled with cheese.

Meat ragout with vegetables

Ingredients:

- Beef steak - 900 g
- Bulgarian pepper colored - 3 pieces
- Large onion bulb - 2 pieces
- Canned tomatoes, peeled - 400 g
- Garlic - 3 slices
- Beef broth - 1 glass
- Light soy sauce - 1/4 cup
- Rice vinegar - 2 tablespoons
- Cornstarch - 2 tablespoons
- Sugar - 1 teaspoon
- Vegetable oil
- Boiled rice, hot

Preparation:

1. Sift the large slow-blowing bowl with vegetable oil. Put on the bottom of the pieces of meat, then chopped Bulgarian peppers, onions, tomatoes and chopped garlic.
2. In a small bowl, mix the broth, soy sauce, vinegar, starch and sugar. Pour this mass of the contents of the slow-blower.
3. Close the slow cooker with a lid and cook the meat stew with vegetables at a slower capacity of 7 hours or at a strong power for 4 hours.
4. Serve meat stew with hot rice.

Pork ribs with beans

Ingredients:
- Pork ribs - 1,8 kg
- White beans, boiled or canned - 425-550 g
- Black beans, cooked or canned - 425 g
- Tomatoes canned in own juice - 400 g
- Wine red dry or water 0.25 cup
- Onion - 1 piece
- Seasoning "Italian herbs" - 1 teaspoon
- Dried rosemary - 0.75 tea spoons
- Black pepper powder - 0,25 teaspoons
- Parmesan cheese grated - 3 tablespoons

Preparation:
1. Cut off all the flesh from the ribs, cut off excess fat. Chop onion.
2. Sprinkle the meat with spices, place it in a bowl of slow cookers. Add onions, beans, tomatoes. Drizzle with wine. Cover and put in the refrigerator for the night.
3. Remove from the refrigerator, put in a slow-cooker. Cover and cook for 8-9 hours at low power or 4-4.5 hours with strong power.
4. Remove the stewed pork and beans in a serving dish. Pour the sauce. Sprinkle with Parmesan cheese.

Chicken wings

Ingredients:
- Chicken wings - 1 kg
- Barbeque sauce - 1 glass
- Apricot or peach jam - 1/3 cup
- Mustard yellow - 2 teaspoons
- Fresh peaches

Preparation:
1. Fold the chicken wings into the slow-blowing bowl. In a small bowl, mix the sauce of the barbecue, jam and mustard, pour this mixture of chicken wings.
2. Close the slow-cooker and cook the chicken wings at a slow rate of about 6-8 hours or on strong power for 3-4 hours.
3. Remove the chicken wings from the slow cooker, place it on a plate and cover to keep it warm. Sauce from the slow cooker pour into the saucepan and put on medium heat, bring to a boil, reduce the heat and stew without covering, about 10 minutes. Serve chicken wings with sauce and peaches.

Spicy chicken wings

Ingredients:
- Chicken wings - 16 pieces
- Chili sauce - 1,25 cups
- Hot sauce - 2 tablespoons
- For cheese sauce:
- Cheese blue - 50 g
- Sour cream 230 g
- Mayonnaise - 1/2 cup
- White wine vinegar - 1 tablespoon
- Garlic - 1 piece

Preparation:
1. Turn on the oven with the grill function for preheating to high temperature. Chicken wings cut thin ends, leaving only fleshy ones.
2. Lay the wings on a baking sheet and place under the grill, fry about 12-15 minutes, until golden brown, turning once.
Put the fried wings in a bowl of slow cookers.
3. In a small bowl, mix both sauce and pour chicken wings on this mixture. Close the slow-cooker and cook sharp chicken wings at low power for 4-5 hours or at strong power 2-2.5 hours.
4. Meanwhile, cook the cheese sauce. In a blender or kitchen processor, load all the ingredients for the sauce and grind well. Pour the sauce into a serving saucepan, cover and put in the refrigerator. Serve hot chicken wings immediately, with cheese sauce.

Burgers with stewed meat

Ingredients:

- Pork without bone - 1 kg
- Mini buns for burgers - 20 pieces
- Ketchup - 3/4 cup
- Onion - 1 piece
- Pepper Bulgarian green - 3/4 cup
- Thyme Dried - 1 teaspoon
- Dried rosemary - 1/2 teaspoon
- Chicken broth - 1/2 cup
- Vinegar Balsamic - 1 glass
- Brown sugar - 1/3 cup
- Honey - 1/4 cup
- Worcestershire sauce - 1 tablespoon
- Dijon mustard - 1 tablespoon
- Garlic - 1 slice
- Black ground pepper - 1/2 teaspoon
- Salt - 1/4 teaspoon
- Cabbage young
- Radish or pickled cucumbers

Preparation:

1. Cut the fat from the meat. Cut the meat into pieces so that they fit into the bowl of the slow cooker. In the slow cooker combine the onions and bell peppers. Top with meat, sprinkle with thyme and rosemary, pour broth.
2. Close the slow-cooker and cook meat for burgers at a slow capacity of 9-10 hours or at a strong power of 4.5-5 hours.
3. In the meantime, pour vinegar, ketchup, honey, Worcestershire sauce into a small sauté pan, add sugar, garlic, salt, black pepper and mustard. On medium heat bring the mass to a boil, then reduce the heat and cook the sauce, without covering, 20-25 minutes, stirring, until lightly thickened.
4. Transfer the meat from the slow-cooker to the cutting board and fork into pieces. Vegetables from the slow cooker are put in a sieve, allow the liquid to drain, and then again transfer the vegetables to the slower cooker along with the meat, add the prepared sauce, close the slow cooker and cook the meat for burgers with vegetables at a slow one hour.

5. Cut the buns in half and fry them in the roast. Serve buns, filling them with meat with vegetables, as well as shredded cabbage and pickles.

Beef with potatoes and rosemary

Ingredients:
- Beef, pulp - 1350 g
- Potatoes red - 450 g
- Carrots - 1 glass
- Onion - 1 piece
- Beef broth - 1,5 cups
- Mustard Dijon - 3 tablespoons
- Fresh rosemary - 2 tablespoons
- or dried rosemary - 1.5 teaspoons
- Fresh thyme - 1 teaspoon (or dried thyme - 0.5 teaspoon)
- Salt - 1 teaspoon
- Pepper black ground - 0.5 teaspoon

Preparation:
1. Wash potatoes thoroughly and, without peeling, cut into quarters. Finely chop onion.
2. Lubricate the bowl with oil. Fold in it potatoes and carrots.
3. In a small bowl, mix mustard, rosemary, thyme, salt and pepper. Grate the mixture with meat.
4. Put the meat on the vegetables, sprinkle with onions. Pour broth so as to cover meat and vegetables.
5. Close the lid. Cook beef with potatoes and carrots in a slow cooker for 8-10 hours at low power.
6. Remove meat and vegetables. Lay out on a serving plate.
7. Remove the fat from the broth. Pour broth beef with potatoes.

Vegetable stew with rice

Ingredients:
- Soybeans fresh - 3 cups
- Batat - 2 pieces
- Carrots - 1,5 cups
- Brown rice - 3 cups
- Vegetable broth - 4 glasses
- Garlic - 3 slices
- Powder curry - 1.5 teaspoons
- Cumin ground - 1,5 teaspoons
- Ground ginger - 1,5 teaspoons
- Coconut milk unsweetened - 3/4 cup
- Cilantro fresh - 3 tablespoons
- Cashew - 1/3 cup

Preparation:
1. Add soya beans, sweet potatoes, carrots, garlic, pour curry, cumin, ginger into the slow cooker and pour everything with vegetable broth.
2. Close the slow-cooker and cook the stew at a slow power for 4.5-5 hours or at a strong power for 2-2.5 hours.
3. Introduce rice into the vegetable mixture and cook the vegetable stew with rice at strong power for about 20-25 minutes, until the rice is mild and the liquid is almost completely evaporated. Then introduce into the slow cooker coconut milk and cilantro. Stir and serve vegetable stew with rice on serving plates with cashews.

Lamb, stewed with beans and artichokes

Ingredients:
- Lamb - 1 kg
- White canned beans - 500 g
- Tomatoes, canned without a skin - 400 g
- Garlic - 6 pieces
- Salt - 1/2 teaspoon
- Oregano dried - 1/2 teaspoon
- Fresh spinach - 3 cups
- Artichokes canned - 400 g
- Orozo paste boiled - 3 cups
- Chees Feta

Preparation:
1. With meat remove excess fat and cut the flesh into pieces about 2.5 cm in size. Fold the lamb into a slow-blowing bowl; pour in the beans, tomatoes, garlic, salt and oregano.
2. Close the slow-cooker and cook at a slow power for about 8-10 hours or at a strong power of 4-5 hours. Then open the slow-cooker and enter the spinach and artichokes, close and let stand for 5 minutes, until the spinach wilt.
3. Serve meat stew with Orzo paste, sprinkled with cheese.

Lamb cooked with vegetables and pearl barley

Ingredients:
- Vegetable oil - 1 tablespoon
- Lamb on the bone - 1.4 kg
- Carrots - 4 pieces
- Stem of celery - 3 pieces
- Tomatoes, canned without a skin - 400 g
- Chicken broth - 400 g
- Pearl barley - 1 glass
- Onion - 1/2 cup
- Water - 1/3 cup
- Black ground pepper - 1/2 teaspoon
- Balsamic vinegar - 2 tablespoons
- Fresh rosemary

Preparation:
1. In a large frying pan over medium heat, heat the vegetable oil. Put on the heated frying pan lamb and fry from all sides until brown. Drain the fat.
2. Put the carrots, celery, tomatoes, croup, onion into a bowl of a large slow cooker, pour the pepper and pour the broth and water. Place pieces of lamb on top.
3. Close the slow-cooker and cook the lamb with vegetables and pearl barley at low power for 7-9 hours, until the meat and cereals are ready.
4. Get the lamb from the slow-cooker and put it on the plates. Remove the fat from the surface of the vegetables. Introduce into the slow-cooker vinegar, mix and lay vegetables with pearl bar on plates with meat. If desired, sprinkle the dish with rosemary.

Chicken fillet

Ingredients:
- Chicken fillet without skin - 6 halves
- Chili powder - 1 tablespoon
- Salt - 1/8 teaspoon
- Chicken broth - 1/2 cup
- Fresh lemon juice - 2 tablespoons
- Chili canned - 1/3 cup
- Cornstarch - 1 tablespoon
- Cold water - 1 tablespoon
- Cream cheese - 230 g
- Bacon - 2 strips

Preparation:

1. Chicken fillet sprinkle with paprika and salt from all sides. Fold the fillets on the bottom of the slow cooker, pour broth and lemon juice. Top with canned chili.
2. Close the slow-cooker and cook the chicken fillet at a slow power of about 5-6 hours or at a strong power of 2 1 / 2-3 hours.
3. Transfer the fillets and peppers to a serving plate, and leave the juice in a slow cooker. Chicken fillet cover with foil to keep warm until serving.
4. In a glass, dilute the starch in cold water and enter into the slow cooker. There also enter the cream cheese and stir well. Close the slow-cooker and cook the sauce on a strong power for about 15 minutes, until thick. Pour the sauce on the fillet on a platter and sprinkle with chicken fillet in a creamy sauce of fried bacon. Serve the chicken fillet in a creamy sauce with any garnish.

Cheese appetizer

Ingredients:
- Mozzarella cheese, smoked - 1 glass
- Parmesan cheese - 0,5 cups
- Cheese creamy - 230 g
- Garlic - 1 slice
- Spinach frozen - 200 g
- Artichokes canned - 100 g
- Salt
- Black pepper powder

Preparation:
Artichokes chop and fold in a bowl of slow-cookers, there also put the rest of the ingredients, salt, pepper. Cook at strong power for 2 hours.

Chicken soup with zucchini and lentils

Ingredients:
- Chicken thighs without skins and bones - 900 g
- Lentil brown - 1,25 cups
- Courgettes yellow - 1 piece
- Garlic - 2 slices
- Cumin ground - 0.5 teaspoon
- Ground coriander - 0.5 teaspoon
- Onion - 1 piece
- Chicken broth - 800 g
- Dried apricots or golden raisins - 0,5 cups
- Green onion

Preparation:
1. In a bowl, mix chicken, garlic, cumin, coriander, cinnamon and 0.25 teaspoons of black ground pepper.
2. Grease a very large cast-iron frying pan with vegetable oil, warm it well. Lay the chicken meat, cook, stirring, until brown on all sides.
3. Transfer chicken meat to a large slow-cooker, add lentils and onions, pour broth and 1 glass of water.
4. Close the slow-cooker and cook at a slow power for 7-8 hours. Then add zucchini and dried apricots, prepare another 15 minutes for strong power. You can serve soup with green onions.

Tomato sauce for pasta

Ingredients:
- Onion medium size - 1 piece
- Ham or bacon - 150 g
- Garlic - 3 slices
- Fresh tomatoes - 400 g
- Tomato sauce with herbs - 400 g
- Dried parsley - 2 teaspoons
- Oregano dried - 1 teaspoon
- Salt - 1/2 teaspoon
- Dried basil - 1/2 teaspoon
- Red pepper dried chili - 1/2 teaspoon
- Pasta orcete or other figured - 8 glasses
- Parmesan - 1/4 cup
- Fresh oregano leaves

Preparation:
1. In a large frying pan on medium heat, fry the ham, onion and garlic until the onion is soft and the ham is crispy. Drain fat from the frying pan.
2. Fry the contents of the frying pan into a slow-cooking bowl, insert cut tomatoes, tomato paste, parsley, dried oregano, salt, basil and crumbled red pepper.
3. Close the slow-cooker and cook the sauce at a slow power for 8-10 hours or at a strong power of 4-5 hours.
4. Serve the pasta with the sauce, sprinkling with cheese and fresh leaves of oregano.

Asian chicken noodle soup

Ingredients:
- Chicken thighs - 450 g
- Carrots - 1 glass
- Red dry wine - 2 tablespoons
- Soy sauce - 1 tablespoon
- Rice vinegar - 1 tablespoon
- Fresh ginger - 1 teaspoon
- Black ground pepper - ¼ teaspoon
- Chicken broth - 320 g
- Water - 1 glass
- Rice noodles - 60 g
- Green peas sugar in pods - 170 g
- Soy sauce

Preparation:
1. Add the chicken meat, chopped carrots, pour wine, 1 tablespoon of soy sauce, vinegar, pour black ground pepper and ground ginger into the slow-cooker. Pour all the water and broth.
2. Close the slow-cooker and cook the soup on strong power for 2-3 hours, then add noodles and green peas, cook chicken soup with noodles for about 3-4 minutes.
3. Serve chicken soup with noodles in a serving sauce with soy sauce to taste.

Sword fish with BBQ sauce

Ingredients:
- Swordfish - 4 steaks
- Worcestershire sauce - 1 tablespoon
- Chile, powder - 0.5 teaspoon
- Sugar cane - 1 tablespoon
- Vinegar balsamic - 1 tablespoon
- Sunflower oil - 1 tablespoon
- Onion - 1 piece
- Garlic - 1 slice
- Mustard - 1 tablespoon
- Tomato juice - 150 g
- Salt
- Black pepper powder
- Fresh parsley
- Lemon
- Boiled rice

Preparation:
1. In a large frying pan over medium heat, heat sunflower oil. Pour the onion into a frying pan, cook, stirring, for about 10 minutes. Add the garlic and chili, cook, stirring, for about 30 seconds. Then enter the Worcestershire sauce, sugar, vinegar, and mustard and tomato juice. Stirring, bring the mass to a boil.
2. Pour half of the sauce into a slow-blowing bowl. Steaks washed and dried on a paper towel, put into the sauce in one layer. Pour the remaining sauce.
3. Close the slow-blower with the lid and turn it on at full power. Cooking fish 2-3 hours, until soft.
4. Transfer the fish to serving plates, pour with sauce and sprinkle with parsley. Serve fish with boiled rice and lemon slices.

Beef tenderloin

Ingredients:

- Beef steak - 1,3 kg
- Carrots of medium size - 6 pieces
- Onion - 1 glass
- Wine red dry or broth beef - 0,75 cups
- Tomato paste - 0,25 cup
- Instant Tapioca - 4 teaspoons
- Worcestershire sauce - 2 teaspoons
- Chili powder - 1 teaspoon
- Ground garlic - 0.5 teaspoon
- Mashed potatoes hot

Preparation:

1. Cut the beef steak into several pieces.
2. Add carrots and onions to the bowl of a large slow-cooker, place pieces of meat on top. In a separate bowl, mix the wine, tomato paste, tapioca, Worcestershire sauce, chili, garlic powder and 1/4 teaspoon of salt. Pour this mixture into a slow-flowing bowl, cover with a lid and cook at minimum power 9-11 hours.
3. Take the meat from the slow-cooker. Vegetables can also be obtained with the help of noise.
4. Serve meat with vegetables and garnish right away, pouring sauce from a slow-cooker.

Spaghetti with meat sauce in Italian

Ingredients:
- Spaghetti - 350-450 g
- Canned tomatoes, in their own juice - 800 g
- Minced beef - 450 g
- Champignons canned - 225 g
- Pepper sweet green - 1 piece
- Tomato paste - 170 g
- Onion - 1 piece
- Garlic - 2 slices
- Laurel leaf - 1 piece
- Seasoning "Italian herbs" - 2 teaspoons
- Salt - 0.5 teaspoon
- Black pepper powder - 0,25 teaspoons
- Parmesan cheese

Preparation:
1. Chop the onions. Garlic chopped. Sweet pepper and cut.
2. In a frying pan on medium heat, fry the mince, onions and garlic until the meat is ready. During cooking, stir the forcemeat with a spoon, so that there are no large pieces.
3. In the slow-cooker bowl, mix tomatoes, tomato paste, mushrooms, bay leaf, Italian herbs, salt and pepper. Add stuffing. Mix. Cover and put in the refrigerator for the night.
4. Prepare minced meat with tomatoes and mushrooms in a slow cooker for 8-10 hours at low power or 4-5 hours at strong power.
5. Remove the bay leaf. Add the sweet pepper.
6. Boil the spaghetti, drain the water.
7. Put the spaghetti on the dish. On top, distribute the meat sauce with tomatoes and mushrooms.
8. Spaghetti with tomato and meat sauce in Italian ready. Sprinkle with grated cheese before serving.

Stew of beef and black beans

Ingredients:
- Minced beef - 350 g
- Black beans, cooked or canned - 850 g
- Tomatoes canned in own juice - 800 g
- Onion - 1 piece
- Pepper Bulgarian green - 1 piece
- Garlic - 3 slices
- Beef broth - 0,75 cups
- Cocoa powder - 2 tablespoons
- Chili powder - 2 tablespoons
- Ground cumin - 1 tablespoon
- Paprika smoked - 1 tablespoon
- Green onion

Preparation:
1. Finely chop onion. Pure the seeds and cut them. Garlic chopped.
2. In a large frying pan over medium heat, fry the mince, onion, sweet pepper and garlic. Cook until meat is ready.
3. Put the meat mixture in a slow-blowing bowl. Add beans, tomatoes, broth, cocoa, chili, cumin and paprika. Mix. Cover and put in the refrigerator for the night.
4. Put the bowl in a slow cooker, cover. Cook at a weak power of 8-10 hours or with a strong power of 4-5 hours.
Stew of beef with beans is ready. When serving sprinkle with spring onions.

Beef with cabbage, carrots and pasta

Ingredients:
- Beef spatula - 1.4 kg
- Cabbage - 0.5 head
- Carrots - 4 pieces
- Vermicelli or thin pasta - 170 g
- Root of ginger - 3-5 cm
- Hoisin Sauce - 0.5 cups
- Soy sauce - 0,25 cup
- Salt garlic - 1 teaspoon
- Pepper black ground - 0.5 teaspoon
- Pepper red - 0.5 teaspoon
- Sesame oil - 1 tablespoon
- Water - 1 glass
- Sesame fried
- Sweet pepper
- Green onion

Preparation:
1. Ginger clean and finely chop. Carrots cut into pieces 2.5 cm, cut into large slices of cabbage.
2. Fry the meat from all sides.
3. Lubricate the slow-blowing bowl with oil. Sprinkle the meat with garlic salt and black pepper. In the slow-cooker, pour in the water, lay out the meat.
4. In a small bowl, mix the hoisin sauce, soy sauce, ginger, sesame oil, flakes of red pepper and the remaining garlic salt.
5. Drizzle the mixture with the top and sides of the meat.
6. Place carrots around the meat. Top with cabbage and carrots. Cover. Cooking meat with vegetables 7-8 hours at low power.
7. Increase power. Gently shift the vegetables to a serving dish, cover with foil.
8. Transfer the meat to the cutting board. Cover with foil and leave for 5 minutes before cutting it.
9. Break the pasta in half. Put into sauce, left in the slow cooker. Stir so that the pasta was completely covered with sauce, cover. Cook with strong power for 10 minutes.
10. Cut the meat across the fibers into slices.

11. Lay the meat and pasta on vegetables. Beef with sauerkraut, carrots and pasta. Sprinkle with sesame seeds and chopped vegetables.

Chicken stewed in tomato sauce

Ingredients:
- Chicken drumsticks and wings - 1 kg
- White canned beans - 350 g
- Salt - ¾ teaspoon
- Black ground pepper - ¼ teaspoon
- Fennel - 1 piece
- Pepper Bulgarian yellow - 1 piece
- Onion medium size - 1 piece
- Garlic - 3 slices
- Fresh rosemary - 1 teaspoon
- Fresh Oregano - 1 teaspoon
- Red pepper - ¼ teaspoon
- Tomatoes - 350 g
- Red dry wine or chicken broth - ½ cup
- Tomato paste - ¼ cup
- Parmesan - ¼ cup
- Fresh parsley - 1 tablespoon

Preparation:
1. Chicken meat sprinkle on all sides ¼ teaspoon of salt and ¼ teaspoon of black pepper. Fold the chicken pieces in a bowl of slow cookers, top with beans, put the fennel, bell pepper, onion, garlic, sprinkle with rosemary, oregano and red pepper.
2. In a medium-sized bowl, combine sliced tomatoes, wine, tomato paste and ½ teaspoon of salt. Pour the contents of the slow cooker with this tomato mixture.
3. Close the slow-cooker and cook the stewed chicken in tomato sauce at a slower capacity of 5-6 hours or at a strong power of 2.5-3 hours.
4. Serve chicken stewed in tomato sauce on a serving plate, sprinkled with cheese and parsley.

Paprikash with noodles

Ingredients:
- Beef - 1,1 kg
- Tomatoes canned in own juice - 400 g
- Bulgarian pepper roasted - 350 g
- Onion - 3 pieces
- Carrots - 1 piece
- Beef broth - 400 ml
- Sour cream 225 g
- Paprika powder - 2 tablespoons
- Corn starch - 2 tablespoons
- Paprika smoked - 0.5 teaspoon
- Water - 0,25 cups
- Butter - 0.25 cups
- Parsley - 1 beam
- Salt
- Black pepper powder
- Noodles - 100 g

Preparation:
1. Cut the onions into half rings. Cut the carrots into large cubes. Pepper cut into strips.
2. With meat cut off excess fat. Cut into pieces. Put into the bowl of the slow-cooker.
3. In a bowl, mix the paprika and the smoked paprika. Sprinkle this mixture with meat.
4. Top with tomatoes and broth. There also send onions, carrots and peppers. Cover and place from evening to morning in the fridge.
5. Place the bowl in the slow cooker. Cook at low power for 9-10 hours.
6. Remove the meat. Using two forks, take out the meat into small pieces. With the sauce, remove the fat from the meat. Add meat to the sauce. Increase the power of the slow-cooker.
7. Mix the starch and water. Pour into meat, mix. Close the slow-cooker and cook for 30 minutes. Add sour cream and spices to taste.
8. At this time, cook the noodles as indicated in the instructions on the package. Drain the water, add oil.

9. Put noodles on a plate, on top - stew in a sauce with vegetables. Cut the parsley and sprinkle the paprika with the herbs noodles.

Meat

Ingredients:
- Beef steak without bones - 450 g
- Tomatoes, canned without skin with herbs - 400 g
- Beer light - 0,5 cups
- Honey liquid dark - 1-2 tablespoons
- Onion - 1 glass
- Vegetable oil
- Salt - 0.25 teaspoons
- Mashed potatoes

Preparation:
1. Lubricate the slow-blowing bowl with vegetable oil, pour the onion into it.
2. Heat a large frying pan over medium-high heat, grease with oil. Put the steak on the frying pan, fry about 3 minutes on each side, until brown. Transfer the steak into the bowl of the slow cooker on the bow. Pour the meat with tomatoes and beer. Close the slow-cooker, cook the meat for a weak power for 8 hours, until the soft state of the meat.
3. Using two forks, break the steak into pieces. Again, put the meat in a slow cooker, add honey and salt, mix, cover, leave for 10 minutes.
4. Serve meat with mashed potatoes.

Sandwiches from ciabatta, chicken fillet and vegetables

Ingredients:
- A mixture of dried Italian herbs - 1 teaspoon
- Salt - 1/4 teaspoon
- Black ground pepper - 1/4 tsp.
- Chicken fillet without skin - 450 g
- Onion - 1 piece
- Mushrooms champignons fresh - 230 g
- Garlic - 2 slices
- Tomatoes, canned without a skin - 400 g
- Red wine vinegar - 2 tablespoons
- Zucchini - 1 piece
- Bulgarian pepper - 1 piece
- Mayonnaise - 1/3 cup
- Pesto sauce - 2 tablespoons
- Bread of ciabatta - 1 piece
- Fresh basil leaves

Preparation:
1. In a small bowl, combine salt, pepper and Italian herbs. With this mixture grate the chicken fillet from all sides. Put chicken in a slow cooker. There also put onions, mushrooms and garlic.
2. In a bowl, combine sliced tomatoes and vinegar, pour the contents of the slow cooker with this tomato mixture.
3. Close the slow cooker and cook chicken at a weak power for 4-5 hours or for a strong 2-2 1/2 hours. Then, put zucchini and Bulgarian pepper into the slow cooker. Cook on strong power for 30 minutes.
4. Meanwhile, in a small bowl, mix the mayonnaise and pesto sauce and apply this mixture to the ciabatta slices.
5. Put the chicken fillets on a cutting board, and put the vegetables on the prepared basic ciabatta cake. Chicken fillet cut into slices and put on vegetables, decorate with basil leaves, cover with a second half of ciabatta and cut the sandwich with chicken for 6-8 servings.

Ragout of pumpkin with turkey

Ingredients:
- Turkey - 700 g
- Pumpkin - 900 g
- Onion - 1 piece
- Beans preserved in tomato sauce - 450 g
- Tomatoes, preserved in pieces, in their own juice - 400 g
- Parsley - 3-4 sprigs
- Vegetable oil

Preparation:
1. Remove the skin from the turkey.
2. Peel the pumpkin from the peel and seeds, cut into cubes with a size of 2.5 cm.
3. Cut the onions into half rings. Grind the parsley.
4. Lubricate the slow-blowing bowl with oil. Lay out and mix all the prepared ingredients, except parsley. Cover. Cooking for 7-8 hours.
5. Take the meat out onto the chopping board. Remove the meat from the bones and put them to the rest of the food, mix.
Stew of pumpkin with turkey is ready. Before serving, sprinkle with chopped parsley.

Stew with chicken

Ingredients:
- Chicken - 1,5 kg
- Tomatoes canned in their own juice - 400-425 g
- Carrots - 0,5 kg
- Onion - 1 piece
- Mushrooms champignons - 225 g
- Broth chicken - 1/3 cup
- White wine vinegar - 2 tablespoons
- Dried rosemary - 1 teaspoon
- Thyme Dried - 1 teaspoon
- Black pepper powder - 0,25 teaspoons
- Vegetable oil - 1 teaspoon
- Boiled noodles

Preparation:
1. Cut the chicken into portions, remove the skin.
2. With tomatoes, drain the liquid, cut the tomatoes into cubes. Cut the carrots into cubes 2.5 cm long. Cut the onions into strips. Wash the champignons and cut into thin plates.
3. Put the chicken in a slow-blowing bowl.
4. In a bowl, mix the tomatoes carrots, onions, broth, vinegar, rosemary, thyme and pepper. Put the mixture on chicken pieces.
5. Close the slow-cooker and cook at low power for 8-10 hours.
6. Before serving, fry in a large frying pan, stirring, mushrooms in oil (8-10 minutes over medium heat), until golden brown.
7. Remove the chicken from the slow-cooker, remove the bones. Chicken meat and mushrooms again put into a stew, mix.
8. Stew with chicken, vegetables and mushrooms is ready. When serving on a plate, put the boiled noodles and top with a vegetable stew with chicken and mushrooms.

Stew of vegetables and meat

Ingredients:
- Spinach leaves - ½ cup
- Fresh parsley - 4 cups
- Mayonnaise - 1 glass
- Tarragon fresh - 1 teaspoon
- Fresh lemon juice - 1 teaspoon
- Fillet of anchovy - 1 piece
- Garlic - 1 slice
- Capers canned - 2 teaspoons
- Ribs beef short - 600 g
- Vegetable oil - 1 tablespoon
- Onion medium size - 1 piece
- Stalks of celery with leaves - 2 pieces
- Leeks - 2 pieces
- Bay leaf - 2 pieces
- Fresh twigs of thyme - 2 pieces
- Garlic - 4 slices
- Pepper black peas - ½ teaspoon
- Small young potatoes - 12 pieces
- Carrots of medium size - 4 pieces
- Turnip medium size - 1 piece
- Chicken drumsticks and thighs without skins - 900 g
- Pork chops smoked - 3 pieces
- Chicken broth - 320 g
- Salt
- Black crumbled pepper
- Dijon mustard
- Pickled cucumbers

Preparation:
. Prepare the sauce. In the water, blanch spinach and parsley for about 1 minute, drain and immediately put into a bowl of ice water for 1 minute, drain and put on a paper towel. Leave the dried leaves of spinach and parsley in the cup of the kitchen processor, add mayonnaise, tarragon, lemon juice, anchovy fillet and garlic, pulsate

until a uniform mass is formed. Transfer the sauce into a serving plate, add capers cover and refrigerate.

2. Remove ribs from the ribs. In a large frying pan on medium-high heat, heat the vegetable oil. Put on the heated frying pan and fry until brown on all sides. Transfer the fried ribs to the plate, and put half the onions in the pan, cut them down, fry until brown on one side, shift the onion to the plate, set aside.

3. Cut the celery stalk into pieces 5 cm, cut off the leaves and set aside. Cut the white part of the leek with 5 cm slices; place the green part of onions aside.

4. Cut a square of 25x30 cm from several layers of gauze. In the middle of the square lay fried onions, celery leaves, green leeks, bay leaves, thyme, garlic and black pepper, peel the ends of the square and tie them together with cotton thread.

5. Put fried celery, white part of leeks, potatoes, carrots and turnips into the bowl of a large slow cooker, lay out ribs, chicken meat and pork chops on top. Also, put a bag of spices in the slow-cooker and fill it with broth.

6. Close the slow-cooker and cook the stew from vegetables with meat at a slow capacity of 7-8 hours or at a strong power of 3.5-4 hours. Remove the spice bag.

7. Serve the stew of vegetables with meat in serving sauces, sprinkle with salt and crumbled pepper. Stew with meat and vegetables are served well with mustard, pickled cucumbers and spinach sauce.

Chicken fillet stewed with vegetables

Ingredients:
- Medium potatoes - 5 pieces
- Pepper Bulgarian green - 1 piece
- Onion - 1 piece
- Chicken fillet - 450 g
- Tomatoes, canned without a skin - 1 1/2 cups
- Ground coriander - 1 tablespoon
- Paprika - 1 1/2 teaspoons
- Fresh ginger - 1 teaspoon
- Salt - 3/4 teaspoon
- Turmeric powder - 1/2 teaspoon
- Dried red pepper - 1/4 teaspoon
- Cinnamon powder - 1/4 teaspoon
- Garlic powder - 1/8 teaspoon
- Chicken broth - 1 glass
- Cornstarch - 4 teaspoons
- Cold water - 2 tablespoons

Preparation:
1. Put the potatoes, Bulgarian pepper, onions and chopped chicken into a bowl of a large slow-cooker.
2. In a medium-sized bowl, combine tomatoes, coriander, paprika, ginger, salt, turmeric, red pepper, cinnamon and garlic, and add broth. Pour this mixture of the contents of the slow-blower.
3. Close the slow-cooker and cook chicken with vegetables at a slow power of 8-10 hours or at a strong power of 4-5 hours.
4. In a small bowl, dilute the starch in water and introduce this mixture into the slow cooker, close and cook the chicken fillet with vegetables on strong power for another 15-20 minutes, until thick.

Chicken Stewed with Vegetables and Herbs

Ingredients:
- Chicken drumsticks - 8 pieces
- Mushrooms champignons small - 225 g
- White onion white - 1.5 cups
- Broth chicken - 0,5 cups
- Red dry wine - 0,25 cups
- Tomato paste - 2 tablespoons
- Garlic salt - 0.5 teaspoon
- Dried rosemary - 0.5 teaspoon
- Thyme Dried - 0.5 teaspoon
- Black pepper powder - 0,25 teaspoons
- Bay leaf - 1 piece
- Wheat flour - 2 tablespoons
- Broth chicken - 0,25 cup

Preparation:
1. Prepare chicken drumsticks, remove skin from them.
2. Put mushrooms and onions in a slow cooker. Pour 0.5 cups of broth, wine, add tomato paste, garlic salt, rosemary, thyme, pepper and bay leaf.
3. Add chicken legs, cover and cook chicken with mushrooms and onions at low power for 7 hours or with a strong power of 3.5 hours.
4. Lay the chicken legs with champignons and onions on a serving dish, discard the bay leaf. Keep the chicken warm.
5. For the sauce, remove the fat from the sauce remaining in the slow cooker. Take 1.75 cups of this gravy. Pour into a small saucepan, put on a stove.
6. In a small bowl, mix 0.25 cups of broth and flour. Stir until homogeneous. Then pour the mixture into the gravy. Cook the sauce, stirring, until thick.
7. Pour the chicken with mushrooms and onions with the resulting sauce.

Spicy beef with vegetables

Ingredients:
- Beef - 900 g
- Cabbage Brussels - 2 cups
- Carrots - 3 pieces
- Onion - 1 piece
- Canned tomatoes - 400 g
- Ground coriander - 1 teaspoon
- Cardamom powder - 1 teaspoon
- Ginger ground - 1 teaspoon
- Turmeric - 1 teaspoon
- Cayenne pepper - 0.25 teaspoons
- Salt - 0.25 teaspoons
- Black pepper powder - 0,25 teaspoons

Preparation:
1. Carrots cleaned, cut into large pieces. Cut the onions with large feathers. Chop the tomatoes.
2. Place the onions and carrots into a slow-blowing bowl. In a bowl, mix tomatoes, cardamom, coriander, ginger, turmeric, cayenne pepper, black pepper and salt.
3. Put the meat on the vegetables, pour tomato mixture. Top with cabbage.
4. Cover and cook at low power for 8-10 hours or at strong power for 4-5 hours. Take out the vegetables and meat.
5. Cut the meat into portions.
6. Serve meat with vegetables hot.

Sandwich with beef brisket and mushrooms

Ingredients:
- Burgers for burgers or ciabatta - 12 pieces
- Breast of beef - 1,3 kg
- Mushrooms champignons - 100-150 g
- Canned tomatoes, in their own juice - 400 g
- Onion - 1 piece
- Garlic - 2 slices
- Tomato paste - 85 g
- Red dry wine - 0,25 cups
- Worcester sauce - 1.5 teaspoons
- Seasoning "Italian herbs" - 1 teaspoon
- Salt - 0.5 teaspoon
- Black pepper powder - 0,25 teaspoons
- Parmesan cheese

Preparation:
1. Champignons cut into plates. Finely chop onion, chop garlic. With meat cut fat. If necessary, cut the meat into pieces.
2. Put mushrooms, onions, garlic in a slow-cooker bowl. Top the meat.
3. For the sauce, mix the tomatoes, tomato paste, wine, Worcestershire sauce, Italian herbs, salt and pepper. Pour the sauce over the meat. Put in the refrigerator for 12 hours.
4. Put the bowl in the slow cooker. Close and cook at low power for 9-10 hours (until soft meat). Take out the meat. Remove the fat from the sauce.
5. If the sauce is too thin, boil it for 5-10 minutes, until it thickens.
6. Grind the meat. Add a little sauce to the meat.
7. Grate the cheese on the grater. Cut the buns. On the lower half lay the meat with mushrooms. Pour the sauce and sprinkle with cheese. Cover the top half with a bun. A sandwich with beef and champignons is ready.

Copyright: Published in the United States by Jane Willan / © Jane Willan All Rights Reserved. No part of this publication or the information in it may be quoted from or reproduced in any form by means such as printing, scanning, photocopying or otherwise without prior written permission of the copyright holder. Disclaimer and Terms of Use: Effort has been made to ensure that the information in this book is accurate and complete, however, the author and the publisher do not warrant the accuracy of the information, text and graphics contained within the book due to the rapidly changing nature of science, research, known and unknown facts and internet. The Author and the publisher do not hold any responsibility for errors, omissions or contrary interpretation of the subject matter herein. This book is presented solely for motivational and informational purposes only.

Made in the USA
Coppell, TX
03 November 2021